FINDING GOD

(in some of the most unusual and unexpected places)

AN ADVENT DEVOTIONAL

Various authors - compiled and edited
by Brian Dolleman

FINDING GOD

Requests for information should go to
brian@northwestleader.com

Published in Seattle, Washington.

Edited by Brian Dolleman & Angela Hagebusch

Printed in the United States of America

ISBN: 1503309703
ISBN-13: 9781503309708

CONTRIBUTING WRITERS

Jason Bentley
April Carter
Micahn Carter
Angie Derrick
Don Detrick
Jodi Detrick
Ashah Dolleman
Brian Dolleman
Doreen Dolleman
Shari Dolleman
Angela Hagebusch
Louise Hoy
Gail Johnsen
Andy Jones
Norm Jones
Kristen Loehrmann
Moses Masitha
Amber Sollie
Tyler Sollie
Bryan Stanton
Kyle Wheeler
Leslie Wheeler
Fr. Ed White

CONTENTS

FINDING GOD

INTRODUCTION

Advent is a time of expectant waiting, holy anticipation, leaning in, and preparing for what is to come. Of course, Christmas marks the arrival of our Savior. In the Gospels, we discover Jesus coming to earth in what is perhaps the most unusual and unexpected way... as a baby, born to an unwed teenage mom, in a small town's barn because there was no vacancy at the inn.

This Advent devotional book attempts to highlight some of the less obvious circumstances and situations in which we discover God at work. It's about finding God – anticipating, looking for, expecting, and awaiting him in unexpected places.

Each devotional has either a question or a challenge and a prayer.

You are invited to lean in, to take the next month or so and give yourself daily to the discovery of God's work in your life.

Happy seeking...

FINDING GOD

Finding God in the Holidays
by Brian Dolleman

Celebrate God all day, every day. I mean, revel in him! Make it as clear as you can to all you meet that you're on their side, working with them and not against them. — Philippians 4.4-5

Jesus celebrated holidays and special occasions. From what I understand of Jewish holidays, they are often multi-day, music-filled, boisterous celebrations with lots of eating, drinking, and dancing.

Jesus didn't avoid the festivities. He participated. In fact, His first miracle was turning water into wine at a friend of the family's wedding. He wasn't a party-pooper who snuck out early; he was a party participant who provided for everyone's enjoyment.

Unfortunately, the holidays do have a way of bringing out the Grinch in us. There are too many gifts to purchase, too many parties to attend, too many family members to endure, too many whining children...

It's easy to get grumpy when we are "supposed to be" celebrating.

And then there are the culture-war generals, taking offense at the term "holiday" in lieu of "Christmas." In their pious attempt to protect and preserve the holiness of Christmas, they strip it of all joy. They guilt-trip us over trees and gifts and reindeer and Santa.

9

I'm sorry, but I just don't see Jesus doing that. Instead, I see Him bringing food, singing songs, laughing and listening, telling stories, entertaining the children, giving extravagantly, staying late... participating in the festivities.

When the holidays become burdensome and you sense your inner Grinch coming to life, remember that Jesus is present in the celebration – not just enduring it, but participating.

Maybe you can't turn water into wine, but perhaps you can be present and actually participate – bringing joy to your friends and family this Christmas.

Question: What do you want your friends and family to get / receive / sense / pick up on from you this Christmas?

Prayer: God, help me to not be a Grinch. I want to be present and participate. Help me to bring joy to others this Christmas. Amen.

Finding God in the Busyness
by Angela Hagebusch

Be still and know that I am God. —Psalm 46.10

Why is it that the last month of the year seems to always be the busiest?

We fill our calendar with gift exchanges, kid's classroom parties, cookie baking and family get-togethers.

There's decorating to be done, presents to shop for, packages to wrap and cards to write.

And between the planning, organizing, shopping, wrapping, celebrating and baking – it can be easy to feel overwhelmed.

We try to squeeze in every last family tradition from decorating cookies to watching all our favorite Christmas movies and in the process we can become so busy that we put the true reason of why we're celebrating on the back burner.

One of my favorite Christmas carols is Silent Night. It's the first two lines of the song that I appreciate the most.

Silent night, holy night, all is calm, all is bright.

How often during the craziness of the Christmas season do we truly take the time to be calm and silent?

Do we ever stop to reflect on how truly holy that night must have been?

11

An angel appearing to shepherds as they watched their flocks, soon joined by a vast host of others – the armies of Heaven, praising God and saying "Glory to God in the highest and peace on earth."

And all because the greatest gift we've ever been given, Christ the Savior, had been born that night in a stable.

I never want to lose sight of what happened that night.

I never want the tree, the lights and the presents to overshadow the real gift we've been given.

During the busiest days of this Christmas season I want to remember to take the time to slow down, to be silent and to give thanks.

I want to make sure my kids know and appreciate why we celebrate the way that we do. I want them to love Christmas for what it truly is, not what I try to make it.

And as a family I want to always be thankful for all we've been given.

Question: In what ways can you slow down and truly appreciate the real meaning of Christmas with your family?

Prayer: God, helps me to not allow the busyness of this season to overshadow the real reason we celebrate. Thank you for the gift You have given us. Amen.

Finding God in the Noise
by Leslie Wheeler

At that time the Roman Emperor, Augustus, decreed that a census should be taken throughout the Empire. All returned to their own ancestral towns to register for this census. And because Joseph was a descendant of King David, he had to go to Bethlehem, David's ancient home. He traveled there from the village of Nazareth. He took with him Mary, his fiancée, who was now obviously pregnant. And while they were there, the time came for her baby to be born. She gave birth to her first child, a son. She wrapped him snugly in strips of cloth and laid him in a manger, because there was no lodging available for them. —Luke 2.1-7

Have you ever been to the state fair on a Saturday? The people, the animals, the music, the carnival games with the workers yelling at you to "step right up", it's NOISY!

This is how I imagine Bethlehem to look and sound at the time of a census. People traveling from all over, merchants on every corner, the town so crowded that a woman about to give birth was given a barn for her lodging.

Speaking of barns, have you ever been in the animal barns at the fair? They stink and the animals never stop making noise.

In the middle of a busy town, in a noisy barn, Mary gave birth to a Savior. Right there, in the middle of complete chaos, the Prince of Peace came to earth.

13

Sometimes my life feels like Bethlehem during the census. My house sounds like a barn in the middle of the night, a crying child, barking dogs and the neighbor setting off fireworks (year round for no reason). I let the noise drown out the voice of my King and I allow myself to be swept up in the chaos.

When I sit down and rock my daughter to comfort her back to sleep and allow myself a moment to look at her tiny features now content in my arms, the noise around me fades. I'm reminded that in the middle of the noise and chaos God scoops me up in his arms just like that and restores peace to my life.

Question: Are you looking for God when the noise is loudest around you?

Prayer: God, when I'm overwhelmed by the noise around me, let me remember that you are right in the midst of it and I can find peace and rest in you.

Finding God in the Celebration
by Kyle Wheeler

That night there were shepherds staying in the fields nearby, guarding their flocks of sheep. Suddenly, an angel of the Lord appeared among them, and the radiance of the Lord's glory surrounded them.

They were terrified, but the angel reassured them. "Don't be afraid!" he said. "I bring you good news that will bring great joy to all people. The Savior—yes, the Messiah, the Lord—has been born today in Bethlehem! And you will recognize him by this sign: You will find a baby wrapped snugly in strips of cloth, lying in a manger." Suddenly, the angel was joined by a vast host of others—praising God and saying, "Glory to God in highest heaven and peace on earth to those with whom God is pleased."

When the angels had returned to heaven, the shepherds said to each other, "Let's go to Bethlehem! Let's see this thing that has happened, which the Lord has told us about." They hurried to the village and found Mary and Joseph. And there was the baby, lying in the manger. — Luke 2.8-16

If there were ever a reason to celebrate it's because the Savior of the world had been born.

The biggest celebration I ever attended was with the entire city of Seattle after the Seahawks won the Super Bowl. The energy was crazy. The excitement and expectancy of cheering on the team in the streets as they drove by was tangible. You couldn't help but get caught up in it.

That can't even begin to describe how it must have felt for the shepherds to at first, be scared half to death by the appearance of an angel - and then, to see an army of angels singing and rejoicing because the Savior had been born. That kind of news demands a celebration.

The shepherds were so excited they couldn't even finish their job. They left their fields and went immediately to find the baby and celebrate with him and his parents.

There is plenty of opportunity to celebrate during the holidays, let's enjoy it and remember the reason we celebrate is Jesus. Let's be so excited about our Savior that we are the life and the light of the party. Be happy, be merry, enjoy the celebration. Jesus is worth the hype.

Question(s): What was the biggest celebration you have ever been part of? How do you think Jesus would like to be celebrated?

Prayer: Jesus, we celebrate you this Christmas! Thank you for coming to us, for being our Savior, and for bringing Good News to the world. Amen.

Finding God in the Decorations
by Andy Jones

There's a classic scene in National Lampoon's Christmas Vacation when Clark Griswold (Chevy Chase) completely loses his mind because his Christmas lights display won't turn on.

His meltdown leads to the assault of some unsuspecting plastic reindeer and to a molded Santa Claus being punched and punted across his yard.

Why? Because Clark couldn't get his display to light up the way he wanted.

Christmas decorations have been part of the joy and wonder of the season for years. For example, the lighted Christmas tree dates back to 18th century Germany.

The evergreen tree symbolizes eternal life and the lights serve as a reminder of hope and joy because Jesus, the Light of the World has come.

It's wonderful to watch little children discover Christmas light displays for the very first time. They often stand in awe of the bright twinkling lights.

"Woooowwww." is a common verbal response kids give when they encounter a colorful display.

Perhaps this was the same response the wise men gave when they spotted the very first Christmas decoration God used to signify the birth of his son.

"And the star they had seen in the east guided them to Bethlehem. It went ahead of them and stopped over the place where the child was. When they saw the star, they were filled with joy!" (Matthew 2.9-10)

Yes, the Christmas star announced the birth of Jesus and led the wise men to find him.

All too often the hassle and pressure of pulling off an impressive Christmas display drowns out the original intent of the symbols.

Did Clark overreact a bit when he couldn't get his lights to work? Probably.

But let's give Mr. Griswold a break. Maybe he was trying to display hope, joy, and peace for his entire neighborhood during the Christmas season.

The lights ought to remind us that indeed the Light of the World has come!

He is our, "Wonderful Counselor, Mighty God, Everlasting Father and Prince of Peace." (Isaiah 9.6)

His light has entered our lives and into this dark world in desperate need of a Savior.

Jesus identified himself as the Light of the World and has asked us to shine just like him.

Challenge: Next time you see a beautiful Christmas display, ask yourself, "How can I shine Jesus' light to the people around me?"

Prayer: God, help me shine. Help me display joy, hope and happiness today and throughout this Christmas season.

FINDING GOD

Finding God in the Distraction
by Gail Johnsen

Fixing our eyes on Jesus, the pioneer and perfecter of faith. —Hebrews 12.2

My husband is the smartest man in the world. He always gets the perfect gift. He learned a valuable secret early in our marriage... he just buys petite and saves the receipt.

If you're like me, the greatest challenge of Christmas is not finding coordinating wrapping paper and bows, it's not preparing the perfect Christmas dinner, it's not even staying within the budget. It's keeping perspective. It's, as they say, keeping Christ in Christmas... keeping focused on the real reason we celebrate. It's even harder to train our children. I believe all of us have been shaped by our consumer culture more than we think.

The reality of missing it hit home when my first-born was 2 years old. He was the first grandchild in the family and the gifts were stacked taller than he was. Waiting for the nod, he began ripping off the wrapping paper faster than I could keep up with him. I tried frantically to help him appreciate each gift... "Oh, it's a truck! Tell Aunt Cheri, 'Thank you.'" "Oh, it's a baseball hat, tell Uncle Glen, 'Thank you.'" On and on it went. It was chaotic. Catching on to my cue, but so caught up in the process, he grabbed the next present, ripped off the wrapping, he held it up and exclaimed, "Oh, it's a box!" and threw it aside. And in the same movement he grabbed the next available present. I knew we'd created a monster.

21

Mesmerized by the wrapping, he missed the gift hidden inside. The tragedy was, for the moment the wrappings satisfied him. And from that time on it has been an uphill battle to keep perspective in our home.

Richard Foster began his classic book, *Celebration of Discipline*, with this appraisal on the condition of American culture: "Superficiality is the curse of our age." Now 25 years later when asked in an interview, "If superficiality is the curse of the modern age, what's the curse of the postmodern age?" His answer: Distraction.

Dallas Willard echoes this sentiment: "The condition of our hearts and our churches today... is distraction. And the fruit of distraction: we don't go in any direction that's worth going in." Keeping our spiritual focus in the midst of so much is a premier discipline of the soul. Otherwise, we will discover one day how lost we've become.

The word "amusement" literally means "to not think." In other words... to be distracted. Like my young son, we become so caught up in the trivialities of our consumer culture with iPods, iPads, satellite TV, electronic games, that we often miss the real gift. Staying attentive in the spiritual life is one of the most difficult disciplines and requires a consistent training of our hearts.

It's a very real temptation in our consumerist society: Rather than seek God himself, we are satisfied with lesser things. Like my young son, we throw aside the One who alone brings abundant life for temporary trivialities only to find disillusionment and disappointment as soon as there are no more gifts to open.

Am I against gifts at Christmas? Certainly not! The giving and receiving of gifts is part of the love we share as families. Let's just keep them in their proper place knowing our possessions do not satisfy the longings of our soul and often distract us from what really matters.

Question(s): Can you think of ways you have been formed by our consumerist culture? What can you do this Christmas season to lessen this?

FINDING GOD

Finding God in the Treasures
by Leslie Wheeler

When you hear the word treasures associated with Christmas don't you think of wise men, magi traveling from the east bringing gold, frankincense and myrrh? I do.
"Jesus was born in Bethlehem in Judea, during the reign of King Herod. About that time some wise men from eastern lands arrived in Jerusalem, asking, 'Where is the newborn king of the Jews? We saw his star as it rose, and we have come to worship him.'" (Matthew 2.1-2)

"They entered the house and saw the child with his mother, Mary, and they bowed down and worshiped him. Then they opened their treasure chests and gave him gifts of gold, frankincense, and myrrh." (Matthew 2.11)

The wise men had made a long journey to bring these gifts to the baby. When they found him, the message bible says: "Overcome, they kneeled and worshiped Him." (Matthew 2.11)

You see, the magi were overcome because they weren't just bringing treasures, they were seeking one. The real treasure of Christmas was not the gold, but Christ himself and they had found him.

We can get caught up in the game of maxing out the credit card to buy the obligatory gifts for people because they might get us something. We must make sure it's of equal monetary value to what they might spend on us, not to mention all the family we need to buy for. If we're not careful, we end up on the other side of Christmas without ever pausing to see the treasure.

Let's slow down.

This year, as we go about shopping for presents, allow those treasures to be a constant reminder of the most generous gift ever given, God's only Son. As we give and receive and watch the wonder in our children as they unwrap their treasures at Christmas, let's be reminded to bow our knee and be overcome by the presence of Jesus.

God can be found in the treasures if you remember to look for him.

Question: Are you taking time to remember the first gift of Christmas as you shop for treasures this season?

Prayer: God, as we bring our gifts in celebration, may we always be seeking the greatest treasure, our Savior.

Finding God In The Dark
by Brian Dolleman

I will give you treasures hidden in the darkness. —Isaiah 45.3

We often use the word "darkness" to describe something that is bad, scary, a threat to our safety, or perhaps even evil. But darkness does not mean God has gone missing. In fact, some of God's best work happens in dark places.

The Bible, in Psalm 139, says God formed you in your mother's womb, and he saw you there - tucked away, hidden in complete darkness. The writer of the Psalm continues, "I praise you because you made me in an amazing and wonderful way. What you have done is wonderful. I know this very well." (Psalm 139.14)

Do you see? Some of God's best work happens in dark places.

When Jesus was born in Bethlehem, the Bible says, "That night there were shepherds staying in the fields nearby, guarding their flocks of sheep." (Luke 2.8)

Jesus – God in the flesh – came to us at night, in the darkness. An angel announced His birth to the shepherds (who were probably the only people awake at the time)...

"An angel of the Lord appeared among them, and the radiance of the Lord's glory surrounded them. They were terrified, but the angel reassured them, 'Don't be afraid!' he said. 'I bring you good news that will bring great joy to all people. The Savior has been born today in Bethlehem, the city of David! And you will find the baby wrapped snugly in strips of cloth, lying in a manger.'

The angel was joined by a vast host of others—praising God and saying, 'Glory to God in the highest, and on earth - peace, goodwill toward all men!'

When the angels left, the shepherds said to each other, 'Let's go to Bethlehem! Let's see for ourselves what the Lord has told us about.' They hurried to the village and found Mary and Joseph. And there was the baby, lying in the manger.

After seeing Him, the shepherds told everyone what had happened and what the angel had said to them about this child. All who heard the shepherds' story were astonished.

The shepherds went back to their flocks, glorifying and praising God for all they had heard and seen. It was just as the angel had told them." (Luke 2.9-20)

Again, some of God's best work happens in dark places.

We can learn from the example of the shepherds in this Christmas story - they listened to God's message to them: "Do not be afraid." And they had faith that God was doing something good – even late at night, even in the dark.

Question: In what ways have you seen God do good things in the darkness?

Prayer: God, help me to not be afraid of the dark. I trust you. Amen.

FINDING GOD

Finding God in the Night
by Angie Derrick

Where is God my Creator, the one who gives songs in the night? —Job 35.10

Questions like this seem to echo in our heads the loudest when its dark and we're tired. When we're tossing and turning in bed. When we just want to sleep but are wide-eyed with worry, guilt, fear, or grief.

Like King David, fasting and praying round the clock for the life of his infant son. (2 Samuel 12.13-19)

Or Jesus seeking God the Father deep into the night in the Garden of Gethsemane, pleading for a way other than the cross. (Matthew 26.36-44)

There are night owls and then there are those whose hearts are wild and awake, hunting desperately for an answer; waiting anxiously for peace.

How do we rest when our hearts are deeply troubled?

When the angel Gabriel told Mary she would be the mother of Jesus, she was young, poor, and unmarried at the time. Mary had many reasons to lie awake at night with worry. And yet, even though Mary's circumstances could have gotten her stoned to death, she exclaims:

"Oh, how my soul praises the Lord. How my spirit rejoices in God my Savior! For he took notice of his lowly servant girl, and from now on all generations will call me blessed. For the Mighty One is holy, and he has done great things for me. He shows mercy from generation to generation to all who fear him." (Luke 1.46-50)

In the face of all the unknowns and hardships that were sure to come, Mary burst into song.

Praise defined the moment.

Like when Jesus, King and Savior of all, was birthed into the stink, grit and discomfort of a stable. Emmanuel - God with us - came into the mess with us, in the middle of the night, small and helpless. Yet the angels couldn't contain their celebration, they couldn't even wait till morning. Instead, the angels lit up the night sky, disrupting it with praise, singing:

"Glory to God in highest heaven, and peace on earth to those with whom God is pleased!" (Luke 2.14)

Glory to God and peace.

Praise is not just an anthem to God – it's a pathway to peace. So don't wait for the perfect time to praise Him. When you're in the thick of your struggles, proclaim His greatness. When chaos is all around you, praise Him for being the same yesterday, today and forever. When your heart is heavy and breaking, sing of his great love.

When everything fails, praise Him – because that is our much-needed "song in the night".

Question: What praise-worthy thing(s) has God done that makes your heart sing?

Prayer: Lord, help me to give you praise even when my troubles keep me up at night. Amen.

FINDING GOD

**Finding God in the Stars
by Andy Jones**

Every August a meteor shower dances its way through our skies. It peaks over a couple nights (usually the 12th and 13th) and it's quite a sight to see.

Sitting out and watching the show reminds us of the wonder of God's creation. It also helps us remember how small we really are.

God chose to use the stars to announce his presence here on earth some 2,000 years ago.

The Star of Bethlehem, also known as the Christmas Star, is one of the most celebrated Christmas decorations.

It's seen atop trees, in department store windows and draws attention wherever it's displayed.

The Christmas star served two main purposes in the Nativity Story:

It announced the birth of Jesus.

"After Jesus was born in Bethlehem village, a band of scholars arrived in Jerusalem from the East. They asked around, "Where can we find and pay homage to the newborn King of the Jews? We observed a star in the eastern sky that signaled his birth." (Matthew 2.1-2)

It led wise men from the east to come and worship Him.

35

"The star they had seen in the east guided them to Bethlehem. It went ahead of them and stopped over the place where the child was. When they saw the star, they were filled with joy!" (Matthew 2.9-10)

Today, the Christmas star serves as an important symbol and reminder to us throughout this special time of year.

God became human for our benefit.

"Jesus has always been as God is. But He did not hold to his rights as God. He put aside everything that belonged to him and made himself the same as a servant... He gave up his important place and obeyed by dying on a cross." (Philippians 2.6-8)

He still leads and guides us in our everyday lives.

"In the Messiah, in Christ, God leads us from place to place in one perpetual victory parade." (2 Corinthians 2.14)

Question(s): Is God still the primary leader of my life? In what ways will I follow Him today?

Prayer: Father, the stars remind me of how small I feel sometimes. Thanks for loving me enough to send your only Son for me. Help me follow you today. Amen.

Finding God in the Quiet
by Brian Dolleman

There is a time for everything. A time to be silent, and a time to break the silence. —Ecclesiastes 3.1, 7

I suspect we are addicted to filling all the spaces with noise.

And when I say "we," I mean us Charismatic Christians – including Pentecostals (who are the worst about this).

Please don't think I'm attempting to throw someone else under the bus. If anything, I'm throwing myself under the bus. I am both a Charismatic and a Pentecostal (although I prefer the Charismatic label, and would like to add a couple descriptors like "gangsta" and "who loves Catholics").

I am constantly working to fill all the spaces with noise – background music, words, videos, more words, and more music.

In a recent conversation about a Sunday service at our church, a friend said:

"This could be taken the wrong way, but my favorite part of the baby dedication was when you guys were all done saying stuff and just stood there for a while holding and looking at her."

Funny how his favorite part was the one without any noise.

FINDING GOD

Maybe we need less cacophony and more opportunities to, as Depeche Mode put it, "Enjoy The Silence."

I do think we need some holy breaks - holy breaks, where we can enjoy the silence. Or listen when nothing is being said. Or actually think for a moment.

I want to work on this in my own life. Hopefully there will be some longer pauses and holy breaks from all the noise.

We usually sing the classic carol "Silent Night" during the candle part of our Christmas Eve services. This song reminds us of the significance of quiet and sleep, peace and rest.

God is present both in the bright light of day and the shadows of night. He is with us when the angels and shepherds throw an impromptu midnight party and he is with us when there are no angels, no shepherds, no songs, and no sounds.

I am convinced that God is in the party, enjoying each moment of celebration – and I believe he is still there when the music stops and everyone else goes home...

And maybe, just maybe, it's in those moments of quietness that He speaks most clearly to our hearts.

Challenge: Make an effort to not fill all the spaces with noise. Plan for some moments of quiet each day – moments to listen and receive from God.

Prayer: God, thank you for being with me everywhere I go. I know that you are still there even when everyone else has gone. Help me to hear your voice when it's quiet. Amen.

FINDING GOD

Finding God in the Field
by Norm Jones

There were shepherds in the fields... watching their flocks at night. —Luke 2.8
When I read the story of the first Christmas I think the most surprised participants had to be the shepherds. The angels knew what was about to happen. Mary and Joseph knew the precious cargo they carried to Bethlehem. The magi knew they were looking for the new king. (The innkeeper doesn't count. He's just a reason to dress one more kid in a bathrobe and sleeping cap.)

But the shepherds, although it was the Jewish Feast of the Tabernacles, were doing what they always did, no holiday for them. To them, this was the same old same old, just another night on the job; watching stinky sheep. There was no announcement in the Bethlehem Star that the Savior was about to be born. They weren't even traveling to report for the census. Their big plan may have been to sneak off for a quick nap after counting the sheep.

Then... Boom! Angels! An ordinary, run of the mill night in the field became a scene of great joy - great joy for all people.

"For unto you is born today a Savior ..."

Certainly, this gave the shepherds something to talk about for years. "Remember the night the angels came and told us about the Savior?" It probably made them a little more excited about heading out to the fields night after night.

I don't have a field. My field is a desk in a cubicle, in a building with row after row of cubicles. Your field may be a drawing table, a tool belt, a classroom, customers to serve, a cash register or a household to manage and you show up for work every day. And you have thousands of times.

In the movie "Return to Me" Marty O'Reilly, played by Carroll O'Conner, tells his granddaughter Gracie, that he is "blessed with work."

Does God bless us with work?

I think so.

Paul told the Colossians "Whatever work you do, do it with all your heart. Do it for the Lord." And for good reason.

Work allows us to use the talents and abilities God has given us.

Work is a means to provide for our families and to be generous with others in need.

Work is where we can show people the kindness of God in real and tangible ways.

The shepherds were surprised when the angel of the Lord appeared to them in the field. We shouldn't be.

Question: When you show up for work, do you ask for, and allow, Jesus to show up too?

Prayer: Lord, today as I work, let me bring honor to your name. Amen.

FINDING GOD

Finding God in the Strange Land
by Moses Masitha

Thus says the Lord, the God of Israel, to all the exiles from Jerusalem in Babylon: "Build houses and live in them; plant gardens and eat what they produce. Take wives and have sons and daughters; take wives for your sons, and give your daughters in marriage, that they may bear sons and daughters; multiply there, and do not decrease. But seek the welfare of the city where I have sent you into... and pray to the Lord on its behalf, for in its welfare you will find your welfare." — Jeremiah 29.4-7

Exile is a place of brokenness, a place of loss and displacement. People in exile never truly feel like they belong. They are always looking over their shoulder, wondering when the source of conflict in their homeland will end, and hopeful that someday they will return to the land where they are most at ease.

To the displaced people of Israel whom God led to Babylon, the Prophet Jeremiah brings a message to be faithfully present even in this foreign land that exposes their strangeness.

Many of us often find ourselves in strange lands that we know are not where we are supposed to be. We find ourselves going through the unfamiliarity of being alone (and for some loneliness), the displacement of being without amenities, the anxiety of not knowing whether we are welcome in the new community we find ourselves in or not. And more often than not we

45

find ourselves wishing this period to be short lived, that it would just be a small valley that we are passing through.

If we are careful to lean in however, we will hear the counterintuitive voice of the prophetic imagination imploring us to plant roots in this strange land. The voice will say to us God has brought us here for a time period and reasons known only to God in spite of our feelings of displacement.

It is interesting when you read through the text in Jeremiah to recognize that this is the first time the prophet has direct communication with the people he had been sent to in the opening verses of the book. And yet, the first comforting thing he says to them is to plant roots in the place of their brokenness and tells them that it is only when they bless this place that it will be well with them.

Maybe God just wants us to be faithfully present wherever we are. Maybe "wherever the soles of our feet shall tread" (Joshua 1.3) includes those areas of our lives that we feel the least in control of and most foreign in.

Question: Have you awakened to the reality of where you find yourself at this moment, be it physically, emotionally and spiritually, and wondered, what does it mean to be faithfully present?

Prayer: God open my eyes to see you and my ears to hear your voice of comfort and instruction even in this strange land.

Finding God in the Center of my Soul
by Fr. Ed White

I love the way Isaiah foreshadows the manger scene right at the beginning of his great prophetic work on the Messiah.

"I have raised and cared for my sons, but they have disowned me!
Even an ox knows its owner, and the donkey recognizes its master's manger; but my people do not know, they have not understood." (Isaiah 1.2-3)

The Lord speaks in this prophecy of how easy it is to know him, and yet how ignorant and unfaithful his people can become.

We run that risk of being distracted and forgetting the Lord, especially during the Advent Season, when commercialism is at full throttle. But we can go against the grain by planning a holy Advent Season of reflection and honoring the traditional Christmas Season.

If God is so knowable, how can we come to know God better during this Advent Season? If there is something in a donkey that recognizes it's master's manger, then surely the Lord has placed within his children, his friends, his beloved and chosen people, the gift to recognize him in our midst, even at our deepest center, where our soul meets God.

St. John of the Cross, writes that:

FINDING GOD

"God is hidden in the soul—you yourself are his dwelling and his secret chamber and hiding place. God is never absent. In order to find Him you should forget all your possessions and all creatures and hide in the interior, secret chamber of your spirit. And there, closing the door behind you, you should pray to your Father in secret. Remaining hidden with Him, you will experience him... and love and enjoy him."

Eastern Christians use a method called the Jesus Prayer...

"Lord Jesus Christ, have mercy on me, a sinner."

They teach us to imagine our heart beating within our chest as we say this prayer, breathing in on the first part "Lord Jesus Christ" and breathing out on the second part, "have mercy on me, a sinner."

The heart of this prayer is the name of Jesus, who took on human flesh, and having a human heart, in order to save us through a solidarity that is intended to be a permanent union of being. He wants to make his home in us.

I challenge you to pray the Jesus Prayer. Try it ten times in a row and see if you don't experience an increase of peace.

While we struggle to find God during the Advent Season, I encourage you to seek him in your soul, your deepest center. Augustine said, "Late have I loved thee, O Beauty so ancient and so new, late have I loved thee. For see, thou was within and I was without, and I sought thee out there." While Christmas hype goes on around us, Jesus waits for us within.

Question: Do I believe and know Jesus living inside of me?

Challenge: Find time to be quiet and alone with Jesus, becoming more aware of his presence in you life, during this Advent Season.

FINDING GOD

Finding God in the Smallness
by Brian Dolleman

The Lord was not in the wind; the Lord was not in the earthquake; the Lord was not in the fire; but instead he spoke in a still small voice... —1 Kings 19.11-12

Why was Jesus born in Bethlehem? The Bible explains...

"At that time the Roman emperor decreed that a census should be taken throughout the empire. Everyone returned to the towns of their ancestors to register for this census. And because Joseph was a descendant of King David, he had to go to Bethlehem, David's ancient home.

Joseph took Mary, his fiancée, with him – and she was now obviously pregnant. And while they were there, the time came for her baby to be born. She gave birth to her first child, a son. She wrapped him snugly in strips of cloth and laid him in a manger, because there was no lodging available for them." (Luke 2.1-7)

"O Little Town of Bethlehem" is one of the most loved and known Christmas hymns. We imagine what Bethlehem might have looked like all those years ago. At the time of Jesus, Bethlehem was a small town of 300-1,000 inhabitants (in comparison, Coulee City, WA has a population of about 500 people).

Today, Bethlehem is a city of 28,000 people in Palestine (this is about the size of Lake Stevens, WA).

FINDING GOD

Bethlehem was, and is, a small town.

And that is where God chose to show up.

We have a tendency to see how God is at work in the big, incredible, flashy, highly-promoted, larger than life stuff – but we struggle to see how God is present in the insignificant, unknown, small stuff.

Throughout His ministry, Jesus did both big and small things. He spoke to thousands and he sat with the Samaritan woman at the well. He attended big dinner parties and he invited himself over to Zacchaeus, the despised tax collector's home.

It's easy to see God in the big.

But maybe He wants us to go beyond what's easy. Maybe He wants us to see (and hear) him in the smallness too.

Question: How have you noticed God in the small things of life?

Prayer: God, I want to see you everywhere. Help me to not overlook your presence and work in the little things and small places. Amen.

Finding God in the Elderly
by Angela Hagebusch

Follow the lead of those who are older. Put on a spirit that is free from pride toward each other... – 1 Peter 5.5

One of the greatest gifts my three children have been given is something you won't find wrapped in shiny paper and placed under the tree.

It doesn't cost anything and can't be bought in a store.

Honestly my children may not even realize the true value of this gift until they are older and have kids of their own.

This gift is the unconditional love of their grandparents and great-grandparents.

These grandparents are modeling not only to me and my husband, but also to our kids what a godly marriage, a loving home and a personal relationship with Jesus truly looks like.

They are present in our lives and are always making sure we are cared for.

And to know my kids are covered in the prayers of their grandparents is a gift in and of itself.

Shortly after Jesus had been born in the stable, Mary and Joseph took him to Jerusalem to be dedicated to the Lord.

While they were there two individuals, Simeon, a good and godly man, and Anna, a prophet, came to Jesus' family.

Luke 2.29 says that Simeon took Jesus in his arms and began to praise God for him, saying "He is a light to reveal God to the nations, and he is the glory of your people Israel!"

The prophet Anna also thanked God for this child and talked to everyone in the temple about him.

Sounds almost to me like two "grandparents" thanking God and showing off this gift of a child.

Growing up I did not have the same kind of relationship with my grandparents that my kids do. But there were plenty of pseudo grandparents from within my church to put an arm around me and encourage me.

What a gift, for the elders in the church to cheer on, love and support the younger generation.

And to cover them in their prayers much like a grandparent does.

In the same way, those who are part of the younger generation should look up to and respect the example of the elders around them who have built their lives around a relationship with Jesus.

Question(s): Who in your life has been a constant support for you? How can you be more encouraging and supportive of those around you?

Prayer: God, help me to be an encouragement to those around me and to model your love for all people. Amen.

FINDING GOD

Finding God in the Young
by Tyler Sollie

For a child is born to us, a son is given to us. The government will rest on his shoulders. And he will be called: Wonderful Counselor, Mighty God, Everlasting Father, Prince of Peace. —Isaiah 9.6

For most of us, the worlds most significant rescue plan would most likely not start with a baby. More likely than not, we would start with something like military power or dominant leadership, not something that seems so small, so weak and so helpless.

But God had a different plan. He came to us and clothed himself with humanity, in the form of a small child.

I love that we are reminded that with His embrace of humanity, he faced the very things we face. The author of Hebrews says, "This High Priest of ours understands our weaknesses, for he faced all of the same testings we do, yet he did not sin." (Hebrews 4.15)

We often think about Jesus as he interacted with the sick and the outcast and brought healing, hope and relationship. We see Him as the incredible teacher that brought together the masses. We see Him taking our place on the cross as our substitute – taking the place that we deserved – to cover our sin.

All of these are vital and very much a part of who Jesus is.

But Jesus was also that toddler who learned to walk. He was the teenager who loved to run, laugh and maybe even sleep in. And through all the changing seasons of life He modeled obedience and trust.

God doesn't just work in the biggest or the strongest. His ability isn't hampered by how smart we are or how many degrees we have. Your current resources, your relationship record or the list of your regrets don't push Him away. You might be young in years or young in trusting Him with your life – and that's okay.

Maybe God never wants us to "grow up" out of our need to trust him.

Maybe that is why His rescue plan started with something that seemed so small.

It becomes easy, the older we get, to approach God out of what we can bring to the equation. But Jesus seemed to continually put a value on approaching relationship with God with a sense of "young".

"Then he said, "I tell you the truth, unless you turn from your sins and become like little children, you will never get into the Kingdom of Heaven." (Matthew 18.3)

It just might be that God never intended for us to grow up out of a place where we trust him like a young child would. Maybe in approaching Him as young, we actually find more than we would have expected.

Question: How can I become more like a child in my faith?

Prayer: God, help me to never grow up out of my need of trusting you. Amen.

FINDING GOD

Finding God in the Stories
by Ashah Dolleman

Since the time I was able to talk, my mom had this digital Christmas book that records me saying something. Every Christmas we record a new 30-second memory (usually my mom prompting me to say something cute and adorable).

When we decorate for Christmas, the digital book comes out from one of the storage boxes and we listen to all the previous year's recordings.

Something happens when we listen to or watch old stories...
Not only are we hearing them with our ears, but they take us back to that time and place. Listening to those snippets refreshes our memories and makes the stories come alive once again.

When I think of Christmas stories, I think of THE Christmas story – the story of Jesus being born in Bethlehem. I'm pretty sure Mary didn't have a digital Christmas book for recording memories with baby Jesus – but I do think she had stories to tell.

After angels led the shepherds to come see baby Jesus, the Bible says that "Mary quietly treasured these things in her heart and often thought about them." (Luke 2.19)

I wonder what kind of stories she told Jesus about that day as he grew up. I wonder if she used the names of the shepherds or angels. Maybe she had a funny story or two about the animals that were there…

We all have stories to tell. I have my own – some are funny, some are cute, some are a little sad. But they show something about me – who I am, where I've been, what I'm all about.

Not only do we discover things about ourselves in our stories, but we also see God at work in our lives.

For me, one of the more personal ways that I can see God is though a story. Listening to God's stories gives me hope and a sense of peace. This is something that we all need in our lives.

The Psalmist said, "I will share with you lessons from our history—stories handed down from previous generations. So let us not hide these truths from our children. We will tell the next generation about the glorious deeds of the Lord, about his power and mighty wonders." (Psalm 78.2-4)

Question: What stories remind you of God's work in your life?

Finding God in the Little Gifts
by Amber Sollie

Every good gift and every perfect gift is from above. —
James 1.17

Wouldn't it be great if we woke up every morning with
a spirit of gratitude and appreciation for all of the gifts
we've been blessed with? Grateful for the gift of today;
another opportunity to make a difference in the lives
around us? Yet, there are days, weeks, even seasons
that it feels as if simply to survive is a victory, and it's
difficult to see the gifts that God has blessed us with.

Have you had an ordinary or even difficult day that was
intersected by someone's kindness or the beauty of
God's creation? The genuine smile of a stranger, the
timely, encouraging text or card sent to you, the police
officer who pulled you over and showed you mercy, the
peaceful stillness of trees covered in frost. When we
slow down enough to be aware of God's greatness, of
his great love toward us, we can see that he uses
creation to gift us daily.

In Psalm 118.24 King David writes, "This is the day that
the Lord has made; let us rejoice and be glad in it."

We can learn from David as he makes this declaration
over his day. He has a spirit of gratitude and is saying,
"God gave me today! I will enjoy it and be thankful for
it!" Our circumstances and our feelings change from day
to day, but God's merciful loving-kindness remains the
same.

God called David a man after his own heart, even though, David went through some of life's most challenging circumstances and was guilty of some of the most serious sins recorded in the Old Testament. His life was full of highs and lows and yet through them all, he sets an example of living a life with gratitude and thankfulness.

"Give thanks to the Lord, for he is good, for his steadfast love endures forever." (Psalm 136.1)

Let's choose to be intentionally grateful for the little gifts in each day. May we be aware of the ways that God speaks to us, through his creation, and to live with such grace toward others that even those who don't yet know Jesus, see the light of his love in us.

Question: What is one of the little gifts that I tend to overlook, but I will choose to be grateful for today?

Prayer: God, open my eyes to the many gifts in my life that are from you, and help me to live with grace towards others. Amen.

Finding God in the Small Town
by Doreen Dolleman

Delight yourself in the Lord and He will give you the desires of your heart. — Psalm 37.4

When our son, Brian, asked me to write something about a small town, I had to smile as I was born, raised, and spent my whole life in Seattle. He reminded me that my husband, Bill, and I had always loved small towns. He was absolutely right! It all started when we were first married and Bill was in the Navy, stationed in Washington D.C.

We often went for Sunday drives, enjoying the peaceful and beautiful countryside. One day we ended up in Amish country in Lancaster County, PA. It was the beginning of years of travels across country to what soon became our favorite part of America. We usually stayed on a Mennonite dairy farm in the tiny community of White Horse and became good friends with many Amish and Mennonite folks.

When Bill retired early at age 50 we just "happened" to be visiting our friends in White Horse. We attended their church one Sunday morning and were surprised at the excitement greeting us when we walked in the door. It seemed that two couples from Washington State were in attendance and surely we had to know each other! Of course, we didn't, but our curiosity was piqued as to why they were there. They told us they were volunteering at Ten Thousand Villages (a Mennonite organization, helping third world countries promote and sell their crafts).

The following day we went on a tour and before leaving had signed up to return to work for three months at their warehouse in small town, Akron, PA. It was a dream-come-true for us, not just vacationing in our favorite little corner of the world, but actually living there.

Every morning we woke up to horses and buggies clip clopping by our house. On Fridays after work we hurried to the local farmers market to buy our Amish dinner. Bonding with the other volunteers led to lifelong friendships. Our volunteer work there and at SERRV, a similar organization in New Windsor, Maryland (another small town) continued for 14 wonderful years, memories we will always cherish. That Sunday at church in White Horse, PA was no coincidence. God surely had his hand upon us and knew the desires of our hearts.

"You've been created for a purpose. I know the plans I have for you. Trust in me." (Jeremiah 29.11)

Prayer: God, thank you for always knowing just how to care for me. Amen.

Finding God in the Poor
by Angela Hagebusch

God blesses you who are poor, for the Kingdom of God is yours. —Luke 6.20

I love the imagery of the Christmas story – the birth of Jesus.

How you have Mary and Joseph traveling through the streets of Bethlehem looking for a place to stay and the only thing available to them is a stable, a barn, a place for the animals.

Luke 2.6 says "While they were there, the time came for the baby to be born, and she gave birth to her firstborn, a son. She wrapped him in cloth and placed him in a manger, because there was no room available in the inn."

So you see, the greatest gift we have ever been given – the birth of a Savior, the One who would later die on the cross for our sins, so that we may spend eternity in Heaven with him – was not born in a palace, wrapped in silk and placed in a gold crib.

Instead He was born in a dirty stable, wrapped in some old cloth and placed in a feeding trough for the animals.

And all this happened for a reason.

It wasn't because Joseph forgot to call ahead and make travel plans or because Mary waited until the very last moment to pack.

No, it's to show that Jesus came for each and every one of us.

From the richest of the rich, to the poorest of the poor – Jesus came for all.

From the person who feels like they've got it all together, to the one who's struggling day in and day out - Jesus came for all.

For the single mom, for the dad struggling to provide for his family, for those who feel completely worthless at times.

Jesus, the King of Kings – came for you – because he loves you.

The Son of God was born poor and even as an adult Matthew 8.20 tells us that he had "no place to even lay his head."

Jesus rode a borrowed donkey, had his last meal in a borrowed room, and his body was laid in a borrowed tomb.

He instructs us to care for "the least of these" and teaches that placing wealth above loving God and others is wrong.

FINDING GOD IN THE POOR

May we learn to see Him in the faces of the poor, the heartbroken, the forgotten - and be reminded that he came for each one of us.

Question: How can you see Jesus in all those around you today?

Prayer: God, help me to remember that every individual matters and is loved by you. Amen.

FINDING GOD

Finding God In The Doghouse
by Brian Dolleman

Since God assured us, "I'll never let you down, never walk off and leave you," we can boldly say, "God is there, ready to help; I'm fearless no matter what. Who or what can get to me?" —Hebrews 13.5

I worked at a veterinary hospital for almost a decade of my life – all during high school, college, and my first year of marriage. It was not glamorous work, but it paid the bills.

The animal hospital has a "front" and a "back." At the front of the hospital there is a waiting area, reception area, and small store with food and accessories. The front of the animal hospital is where most of the people are.

The back is a completely different story. This is where the kennels are - which house the cats and dogs and the occasional guinea pig or bunny. There is a surgery room, an X-ray room, a bathing and grooming room, fenced dog runs, and an isolation ward for the really sick animals. The back of the animal hospital has more animals than people. It's noisy – but not with words we would understand. Instead, you hear loud barking and meowing and even some growling.

I always felt safer working in the back than in the front when I worked at the animal hospital. As bad as cat scratches and dog bites are, the real danger came from their owners. Dealing with the people was always a greater challenge than dealing with their pets. People would often be rude and insulting, and at times would even threaten us.

But among the kennels and the animals that occupied them, I often felt God's presence. In those various veterinary hospital rooms, I would reflect on the goodness of God, whisper prayers, and sometimes even receive God-inspired ideas and dreams.

God is present, even in some of the most unexpected and unlikely places. Yes, even in the doghouse, God is there.

Jesus was born in a barn and placed in a manger – an animal feeding trough. We sometimes think of places or situations as godforsaken or godless. But I'm not sure there are any godforsaken places or godless situations.

Remember what the prophet Isaiah had to say about the coming Savior? "The virgin will conceive a child! She will give birth to a son and will call him Immanuel (which means 'God is with us')." (Isaiah 7.14)

God is with us, in every place and every situation. He's with us on the scenic mountaintops of victory and the deep dark valleys of defeat. He's with us in the front of the hospital and the back. And He is present in the big house and in the doghouse.

Challenge: Make it your habit to think about God and talk to him in "unusual" places, not just the "usual" ones.

Prayer: Jesus, thank you for being God WITH us. Help me to sense your presence and hear your voice everywhere, including some of the most unusual places. Amen.

FINDING GOD

**Finding God in the Presence of Shepherds
by Andy Jones**

Being a shepherd must be a stinky and difficult job.

You herd animals all day long. You live and work among them. Their smell becomes your smell. When you go home at night you bring the herd with you in the form of a wafting odor.

It's a job that must get done, yet probably isn't celebrated or valued much.

It's curious to note how God chose this group, this stinky blue-collar crew, to be the first to learn the arrival of his one and only Son.

Suddenly, an angel of the Lord appeared among them, and the radiance of the Lord's glory surrounded them.

"I bring you good news that will bring great joy to all people. The Savior—yes, the Messiah, the Lord—has been born today in Bethlehem, the city of David!

Suddenly, the angel was joined by a vast host of others—the armies of heaven—praising God and saying,

"Glory to God in highest heaven, and peace on earth to those with whom God is pleased."

When the angels had returned to heaven, the shepherds said to each other, "Let's go to Bethlehem! Let's see this thing that has happened, which the Lord has told us about." (Luke 2.9-14)

FINDING GOD

The shepherds must have been shocked at what they saw and heard for so many reasons.

For starters, what a show! Angels. Lots of them. Singing. Great news.

And most of all God's presence. Right there in the fields where they worked day and night.

God could've chosen anyone and anywhere to announce the birth of Jesus – and he chose a group of working class common men.

They weren't royalty. The good news wasn't saved for an audience at a pristine palace.

It underscores exactly what the angels said, this is, "Good news that will bring great joy to ALL people."

By announcing this incredible news to people viewed as simple and low-class God also demonstrated the accessibility of our Savior.

The shepherds recognized God was talking to them. How humbling. How incredible.

Their natural response was to share the good news that had been shared with them.

Question: How have I been guilty of excluding others based on personal preference?

Prayer: God help me share your good news with ALL people and not reserve it for only a privileged few.

FINDING GOD

Finding God in the Barn
by Don Detrick

The first thing you notice is the smell. As you open the barn door, you are greeted by a pungent fragrance concocted by an assortment of livestock and their waste products that blankets the air. At the same time, hay, grain, and seasoned wood all exude a pleasant bouquet. It is the other stuff that packs a punch. The ammonia-laced chaotic mingling of scents nearly knocks you off your feet. The aroma is not something twenty-first century nostrils in the western world are accustomed to. Reactions vary from a gag reflex to, "Oh my, how do you ever get used to this?"

"Well, it is just all part of the organic process," your farmer host might explain. "You do get used to it, and hardly even notice after a while."

"Why would anyone want to get used to this?" you silently ponder.

Covering your nose with your shirt sleeve to recover from the assault on your nostrils, your eyes begin to adjust to the light and take in your surroundings. Dusty cobwebs, a rat scurrying across the rafters, and steam rising from a nearby cow pile trigger your fight or flight response.

Even if you are not a germaphobe, your thoughts race toward the viral-bacterium spectrum. E coli and other unpleasant words that start with an "e" like, "epidemic" make you wish you had brought along a face mask and rubber gloves. If you are a germaphobe, especially a germaphobe mother, you are planning your escape route. Organic this place may be. Sanitary it is not.

"Thank God I don't have to live in a place like this!" you whisper. And God whispers back, "I chose a place like this to deliver my Son into the world."

Why would God choose such a location? While there are many Old Testament prophecies to explain the intricate details of God's plan, here is the simple truth. Jesus was born in a stable, a place where lambs were born while shepherds watched, for reasons that go beyond sanitation, ambiance, or aroma.

Bethlehem was the home of David, the shepherd who wrote, "The Lord is my shepherd." (Psalm 23.1) What more appropriate place for, "the Lamb of God, who takes away the sins of the world" to be born? (John 1.29, 36)

Shepherds represented common, ordinary people without position or privilege in the world. They found Jesus in a barn. Jesus finds us and receives us, overcoming our smelly mess and chaos with the sweet fragrance of his love.

Where will Jesus find you today? Where will you find Him? And will you reveal Jesus' presence to others as the shepherds did? God is with us wherever we are, even in a barn.

Prayer: Jesus, I thank you for finding me. Help me to both notice you and share you with others today.

Finding God in the Manger
by Louise Hoy

And while they were in Bethlehem, the time came for her baby to be born; and she gave birth to a first child, a son. She wrapped him in a blanket and laid him in a manger, because there was no room for them in the village inn. — Matthew 2.6-7

Mary gasped as a sharp pain spread across her belly. Joseph, alarmed, ran back to the innkeeper and begged for any shelter. Here they were in Bethlehem, after a week of hard travel and there were no rooms. Not one! She leaned against the wall all the while asking herself, where is that favored state the angel promised? Am I to have my baby in the street?

Joseph dashed back and half carried her to an animal shed around the back. She let out a little sob, cut short by a contraction, then gasped, "Is this to be my birthing room, here with animals? We have no crib for our baby. Haven't we done everything God has asked? It's not right!"

But the baby would not wait... Joseph helped her and soon the little one was in her arms and they named him Jesus. Joseph dragged over a feeding trough, cleaned it out as best he could, and they wrapped the baby in a blanket and laid his sweet form in the manger so they all could rest.

Can you relate to this story? Do you feel as if you are in the shed, improvising with a feeding trough, asking why

God has forgotten you and why things are so bad when you've done all you know to stay on the right path? If so, don't forget the rest of Mary's story. Armies of angels proclaimed good news. Devout rulers showed up with gifts. God protected the family from an evil governor. Jesus became a wonderful child who always looked after his mom. Plus, He was the Savior of the world.

Prayer: Dear Jesus, help me remember that following you may not be predictable or look like what I expected. Help me to believe in your promises and your unending great love for me. Amen.

Finding God in the Aromas
by Norm Jones

For we are the aroma of Christ to God among those who are being saved and among those who are perishing. —2 Corinthians 2.15

Don't you love the smell of Christmas? Candy canes, the pumpkin pie with a cup of coffee, a fresh cut evergreen, cookies baking, turkey roasting, cinnamon, cloves, and the genuine cowhide leather of a Regent Bobby Shantz Signature baseball mitt ...

That one's for me. Greatest gift ever. I slept with that mitt, held it over my face, breathing in the smell of the oily leather, dreaming of the glory that awaited me come spring and feeling loved.

You see, God has designed us in such a way that our sense of smell pulls up memories almost instantaneously. Our olfactory bulb is part of the brain's limbic system, our "emotional brain." The olfactory bulb has easy access to the amygdale – which processes emotions and the hippocampus which is responsible for associative learning ... okay, too technical.

Still, our sense of smell is as important to our celebration of Christmas as the shimmering lights, the hand-me-down ornaments, the tastefully gaudy decorations, (hopefully) snow and the sounds of children laughing and joyful music (despite too many renditions of a song about a little boy who thinks a drum solo is the perfect gift for a newborn baby).

83

FINDING GOD

The aromas of Christmas can take us immediately to what we knew as times of quiet joys with friends, boisterous, fun times with family, our grandparent's house and of home; places where we were wanted, accepted, welcomed and loved.

The Bible tells us that we are the aroma of Christ to the world; to those who know Jesus and those who don't.

Among believers, our lives should be a source of encouragement and a reminder of the wonderful and forgiving God we serve.

To those who don't believe, the aroma should be drawing them into the arms of Jesus; the merciful, grace filled arms of Jesus.

But, it has to be real. A friend told me of her son's disappointment when he came in the door thinking sugar cookies were baking and it turned out to be just a scented candle.

The sweet fragrance of a real, full life – a life changed by grace - should flow out through our words, attitudes and actions.

Question(s): Is the aroma of Christ flowing from us? Do the people who walk through our doors sense they are wanted, welcomed, accepted and loved? Do they know they're home?

Prayer: Lord, your word says we are the aroma of Christ to the world. Help us to be the true fragrance of grace, mercy and love. Amen.

FINDING GOD

Finding God in the No Vacancies
by Jodi Detrick

It's true. I'm a complete pushover for signs. No, not the stop-go-yield kind that direct traffic. As a bonafide word-nerd, I'm drawn to the wise and witty combination of words that some sign-ster has framed, in fancy font, upon a backdrop of paper, wood, or metal. Recently, I meandered through a quaint little shop reading signs of all kinds, strategically-placed to catch the buyer's eye. Some of my favorites were:

"Never kiss a fool or be fooled by a kiss."

"Don't you wish we could throw ourselves in the dryer and come out unwrinkled and two sizes smaller?"

Oh, yeah. Those made me smile, but some signs I've placed on the walls of my own home over the years make me think:

"A heart in love is always young."

"What people need is a good listening to."

"When your heart speaks, take good notes."

Signs guide our lives and help us find our way. We would be lost, literally, without them. Still some are certainly less welcome than others. I've never seen, "Hazardous Waste" or "Road Work Ahead: Expect Delays" hanging on anyone's living room wall.

FINDING GOD

"No Vacancy" is another jarring sign, especially when you're weary and desperately need a safe place to lay your head. But as part of the human condition, we bump up against No Vacancy signs, in one form or another, all our lives.

A third-grader swallows hard and blinks back tears when he's turned away from a seat at the table by fellow-classmates who snicker as he carries his crumpled lunch sack to a lone spot in the cafeteria.

A teenage girl dresses in all black, always, to match the despair of being pushed away by a mother with vacant eyes and a drink in her hand, always.

A high school senior groans as he reads the letter of rejection from the university he's wanted to get into since eighth grade.

A young couple hold each other and sob. Infertility, it seems, has put a No Vacancy sign on the door to parenthood and their brightest dreams.

Life after No Vacancy leads us to a place of "instead," an unwanted land, but one where we struggle, grow, and encounter grace in a new way.

Here's the thing. Jesus knows all about No Vacancy signs - it was his first earthly experience: "And while they were there, the time came for her to give birth. And she gave birth to her firstborn son and wrapped him in swaddling cloths and laid him in a manger, because there was no place for them in the inn." (Luke 2.6-7)

I wonder, when Joseph and the very-pregnant Mary faced their No Vacancy night, did they have any idea they were being re-routed by God to a humble place of wonder - a place that, unlike the inn, could host awestruck shepherds under a sky of celebrating angels? How could they fathom that millions of us would place a crèche, the miniature facsimile of their "instead," in our homes every Christmas season? Did they understand that disappointment would ultimately birth delight?

No Vacancy never means no hope. It is a sign where, if we are looking, we will find God, instead.

Question: What is the biggest No Vacancy sign in your life lately?

Prayer: Dear God, please help me to find you in the No Vacancy places of my life. Help me to find peace, and even joy, in my own "instead," knowing you are there with me. Amen.

FINDING GOD

Finding God in the Taxes
by Andy Jones

"In this world nothing can be certain, except death and taxes." —Benjamin Franklin is credited with this uplifting quote.

In a world with very few certainties these two remain constant.

Such was the case when Jesus was born into this world. His mother and earthly father were being summoned back to Joseph's hometown to register for the census and pay taxes.

"All returned to their own ancestral towns to register for this census. And because Joseph was a descendant of King David, he had to go to Bethlehem in Judea, David's ancient home. He traveled there from the village of Nazareth in Galilee." (Luke 2.3-4)

The Bible gives us these details to remind us that Jesus was born into normal, average and humble circumstances. His parents were not elites; they were subject to human authority and didn't receive any special treatment.

It's rare to find a people group at any point in history that feels under taxed. The Jews in Jesus' day were frustrated with the Roman taxes they had to pay. For some this led to violent protests.

People hoped Jesus would rescue them from the oppressive Roman rule. Jesus demonstrated on multiple occasions that he was building a different kind of kingdom, an eternal one.

Jesus lived and ministered in a day in age in which taxes were part of the culture. Even the Pharisees tried to use the issue of tax-paying to trap Him during his ministry.

Jesus wouldn't take the bait. When asked if it was lawful to pay taxes or not Jesus responded with, "Give to Caesar what belongs to Caesar, and give to God what belongs to God." (Mark 12.17)

If Jesus didn't exempt himself then why should we?

While we don't celebrate taxes they do serve as a reminder that we belong to one another. Collectively, taxes pay for the roads we drive on, the schools our children attend and the police that serve and protect us. Together we reap the benefit and together we contribute.

Are taxes something we look forward to? Probably not, but they're part of the world we live in.

How do we find God when it comes to taxes? Maybe taxes serve to remind us that we are part of this world and subject to its laws and authority. Yes, someday we'll move on to an eternal kingdom, but until then Jesus reminds us to participate lawfully in our current system.

Question: In a world of death and taxes, how will you see God at work in your life today?

Prayer: God, remind me today that I belong to others in my community - and how they also belong to me. Amen.

FINDING GOD

Finding God in the Broken Places
by Brian Dolleman

He heals the brokenhearted and bandages their wounds.
—Psalm 147.3

Aaron Kunce wrote something on Twitter the other day that captured my imagination…

When Jesus went about his work in the carpentry shop
I wonder which work he loved the most
creating new pieces…
or restoring old ones.

What a fun question. Of course we don't really know the answer. Jesus certainly was involved in creation (John 1.3). It also seems as though much of His earthly ministry was about healing, restoring, and bringing freedom to those who were oppressed.

One of God's specialties is restoration. He invites the sin-stained. He welcomes the brokenhearted. He receives the imperfect with open arms.

So we come—broken, stained, and scarred. And He does what only he can do. He revives. He restores.

I bought a 1968 VW Bus for $300 when I was in high school. It was a project—a real fixer-upper. The engine was in bad shape, so I asked my mechanic to put in a bigger, better engine.

The mechanic's bill: $1200. Expensive.

I decided to tackle the bodywork and paint myself. So I sanded the entire vehicle down to the metal, inside and out. I started using lots of Bondo (a putty for patching-up dents and holes). And this is where I got stuck.

The bus was nowhere close to being ready for paint. Parts were scattered everywhere and I couldn't remember where most of them belonged. I had no idea how to finish the project. I didn't have the resources. I was out of money, expertise, and motivation.

It was time to put the bus project on hold. Eventually, I came to the realization that I could never complete this project.

I sold my sanded-down, disassembled VW Bus...
For $300.

It's frustrating and embarrassing to think about it. I was overly ambitious and optimistic. I was in over my head. I lacked the knowledge, resources, and ability to get the job done.

I was unable to restore the bus.

My tale of the VW Bus "project" is one of failure.

Obviously, there is someone else who is better at restoration projects than me. I'm not talking about cars now—but our fixer-upper, restoration project lives.

God is the ultimate restorer. He lacks nothing. He has the ability, resources, expertise, motivation... He has what it takes to get the job done.

FINDING GOD IN THE BROKEN PLACES

"God, who began the good work within you, will continue his work until it is finally finished..." (Philippians 1.6)

I love this. God doesn't give up on us. What he started in us—he is faithful to complete. God restores, start to finish.

Prayer: God, I trust your restoring work in my life. What you started, you are faithful to finish. Thank you for making me into the person you want me to be. Amen.

FINDING GOD

Finding God in the Sorrow
by Angela Hagebusch

I weep with sorrow, encourage me by your word. —
Psalm 119.28

Christmas should be a time of laughter and celebration, a time to spend with family and friends.

For some however, Christmas can feel more like a time of sorrow and sadness.

When I was 16 years old, Christmas looked nothing like it had all the years before.

My dad, who had been in a motorcycle accident 4 months prior, was still living in a rehabilitation hospital due to the brain damage he had sustained during the accident.

And my mom, who had just undergone an extensive surgery to remove the cancer that was in her body, was incredibly sick and weak.

Lights were not put up on the house that year and most of the ornaments did not make it out of the box.

Christmas morning there were no gifts in the stockings or large presents under the tree from Santa; instead just a few small things I had bought the day before.

My brother picked my dad up from the hospital that morning and we all spent a quiet day together as a family.

FINDING GOD

I heated our dinner in the oven and we sat in the family room on the couch with TV trays to eat rather than the dining room table because it was more comfortable for my mom.

That Christmas looked nothing like it had all the years before.

It was the most humble Christmas I have ever experienced.

And all that mattered after a very difficult and trying year was that we were all together.

It was also the last Christmas I would spend with my mom – as she died a month later.
Christmas has never been the same for me since that year.

And although each year I miss her dearly, and wish so desperately that she could be a part of our celebrations – I choose to not let the sorrow overrule my happiness.

It can be difficult to look past the pain we experience, but remembering that God is at work even in the midst of it can cause us to once again find joy.

Trust in God's plan.

Seek Him in your sorrow.

And rely on His faithful promise for bright and beautiful days ahead.

Question(s): Have you let sorrow overrule happiness in any area of your life? How can you change that?

Prayer: God, help me to keep my eyes on you and to rely on you during my pain. Amen.

FINDING GOD

Finding God in the Pain
by Bryan Stanton

We all experience pain in our lives. It is an experience common to everyone. Some times (hopefully most of the times) they are minor pains that are expected or can be considered the natural byproduct of a string of events, like getting a ticket for driving too fast, or breaking a finger while playing softball at the company picnic. Sometimes they are more personal, and hurt on a deeper emotional level, like when we lose a loved one after a long illness, or a divorce after a tumultuous marriage. These pains we understand, and although they may be difficult to deal with at some level, it is not too difficult to find a place of peace and confidence that God has all things under control and that we can trust him to get us through.

There are pains, however, that catch us completely unaware, don't seem to make any sense, and even challenge the core of our relationship with God. Pains so great they take our breath away and make it difficult to swallow. The death of a child, the unexpected cancer diagnosis, a terrible accident – they leave us feeling hollow, empty, alone, and asking God, "How could you let this happen? Where are you?"

It is a legitimate question of the skeptics, "How can a loving God allow injustice and seemingly meaningless pain to befall innocent people?" The answer comes easily, until you find yourself face to face with pain that has you paralyzed, feeling stunned and alone, wondering how God could have let this happen to you.

103

FINDING GOD

When we feel we need to have some answers to make sense of it all so we can begin to go on, heaven seems silent, and all of the love and encouragement we get from fellow believers, though received gratefully, does not seem to soothe the pain.

We resign ourselves to the truth written in Isaiah 55.8-9:

"For my thoughts are not your thoughts, neither are your ways my ways, declares the Lord. For as high as the heavens are higher than the earth, so are my ways higher than your ways and my thoughts than your thoughts."

But that doesn't help, not really. That can seem to paint God as a distant, impersonal string puller that is not bothered with the mundane details of my insignificant life. We have well-meaning friends who try to encourage us with Romans 8.28:

"And we know that God causes everything to work together for the good of those who love God and are called according to his purpose for them."

A truth we can, and must, hold on to in our desperation, but one that does not answer that base question, "Where are you in all of this God?" Surely His plan could have been accomplished in some other way...

It is in these moments we must look upon a hill outside the City of Jerusalem. A hill that from a certain angle resembles a human skull. On that hill we see three crosses, and on those crosses, three men. Two are thieves and insurrectionists, criminals, we could say they deserve to be hanging there. But the one in the middle is not like them. He has harmed no man, he is without sin.

He is the Creator of the Universe and he hangs there, naked and bleeding after being beaten mercilessly. In His agony and pain we hear him cry out, "My God, my God, why have you forsaken me?" And we realize He knows exactly how we feel. He understands that hollow empty feeling inside and the feelings of intense loneliness, for he has experienced it.

He has shouted out his questions to a God who does not seem to be listening, confessing his doubts without abandoning his faith. He knows... he gets it... and he is there, right beside me - not offering to answer my questions, but to let me know he has never abandoned me. So I know I can make it - because He is there, and my love for him deepens.

"So then, since we have a great High Priest who has entered heaven, Jesus the Son of God, let us hold firmly to what we believe. This High Priest of ours understands our weaknesses, for he faced all of the same testings we do, yet he did not sin. So let us come boldly to the throne of our gracious God. There we will receive His mercy, and we will find grace to help us when we need it most." (Hebrews 4.14-16)

FINDING GOD

Finding God in the Unmet Expectations
Shari Dolleman

I remember crying into my pillow, feeling like a failure that I couldn't give my parents a grandbaby. I felt passed up by others who easily got pregnant, or didn't intend to. On Mother's Day in church I fought back tears when mothers were presented a rose. I would cry as I cross-stitched gifts for pregnant friends and family members...

Jealously, envy, disappointment and anger felt like frequent visitors.

I'd love to report that the grieving over the inability to add to our family wrapped up in a few weeks or months. But it didn't. I actually feel like different aspects of the grieving went on for ten years.

So while I'm embarrassed to say that the struggle was so real for so long, I also love to expose this – in the hope that it gives others hope. Grief is such a personal thing - and it can take a lifetime.

When I realized that God was with me in all of this— that he was longing to comfort and heal me, I felt like that was a moment of being freed from the years of unmet expectations.

In my unmet expectations I found God. I could see that He hadn't abandoned me, but was with me.

FINDING GOD

My understanding shifted as I realized that God wasn't the one who wanted to withhold good gifts from me, but he was the one who came alongside me in my sadness to be present in my pain. It's like He wanted to sit next to me on my couch and wrap me up in a big warm blanket and let me cry it out. He'd listen and tell me how it wasn't fair, and that he cared, he loved me and he was sorry that I was hurting so much.

When I see the suffering He endured - no wife, no children, being betrayed, being unjustly criticized and killed - I realize he gets me. He can understand my pain, and it is significant to him.

One of my favorite verses is 2 Corinthians 1.4 because it reminds me that God comforts me so that someday I can comfort others with the same care I've received from him.

I'm hoping that even in my example of unmet hopes you might be encouraged to know that your story matters to God. Your pain is real. You deserve to be heard. You don't have to hurry up and get better. Take all the time you need. We have a patient and "God with us" kind of Savior.

Prayer: God, thank you for being with me in my pain, disappointments, and unmet expectations. I need your comfort today. Amen.

Finding God in the Blended Family
by Micahn Carter

For a long time what I thought was a curse was actually a blessing.

I am a product of a relationship that never resulted in marriage. My father is black and my mother is white.

On my mother's side of the family I'm the youngest of three. She had two other children from a previous marriage. On my father's side of the family I'm the second oldest. He had three other children from other relationships. With both sides combined I'm smack dab in the middle. And to top it all off I'm technically an only child. I don't have any other family members that share the same DNA as me. All of them are all half brothers and sisters.

Blended... I know all about it.

It's hard to explain the feeling of trying to fit in to a system with no other components like you.

I would often feel insecure and forgotten. Lost in the mix.

But what if the thing I was struggling to embrace was really what God was after all along.

After all, everything that ever existed started with a blended family. The Father, The Son, and the Holy Spirit.

109

Jesus himself was born into a blended family. He was fully God and fully man with no siblings to share his DNA, while being raised by a man who was not his biological father.

Maybe blended isn't a bad thing.

Every family one way or another starts out as blended.

A man and women from two different backgrounds come together to create something beautiful that only can happen when things become... blended.

Look around.

What's a painting without blended colors and textures?

What's a recipe without blended ingredients?

What's a song without blended instruments, sounds, and voices?

It's easy to see the beauty of things that become blended in almost every other arena of life.

The enemy wants you to become insecure, confused, and isolated, but God is always trying to bring things together.

No matter what situation you find yourself in; married, divorced, remarried, step kids, stepparents, adopted, foster kid/parent, interracial, or any other blended concoction, He is right there in the mix.

He knows what needs to be blended to create the perfect you. Your song will be beautiful let Him choose the sounds.

"In Christ's family there can be no division into Jew and non-Jew, slave and free, male and female. Among us you are all equal. That is, we are all in a common relationship with Jesus Christ. Also, since you are Christ's family, then you are Abraham's descendant, heirs according to the covenant promises." (Galatians 3.28-29)

Question: What are some ways you can embrace your uniqueness?

Prayer: God, help me to embrace what you are blending in my life. You know what you are doing. Amen.

FINDING GOD

Finding God in the Changed Plans
by Jason Bentley

Now after Jesus was born in Bethlehem of Judea in the days of Herod the king, behold, wise men from the east came to Jerusalem, saying, "Where is he who has been born king of the Jews? For we saw his star when it rose and have come to worship him." And being warned in a dream not to return to Herod, they departed to their own country by another way. —Matthew 2.1-2, 12

Historians note that leading up to the birth of Jesus, there was a universally pervasive feeling that something significant and monumental was about to happen. Therefore, can you imagine the worldwide stir after a heavenly body showed up matching the description of ancient prophecies?

As a result, Matthew records that some astrologers in the east made plans to follow the star, worship the royal child, then spread the good news about His location.

We're not that much different than those men. It doesn't matter if our plans are the result of wishful expectation, facts, or a spiritual prophecy, we predetermine what we are going to do and how things are supposed to go. However, plans change. The wise men had to go home a totally different way.

So, there are two things we should keep in mind when plans change:

1. Those that have the faith to be flexible never get bent out of shape.

If you can trust God enough to adapt to the sudden changes life inevitably brings your way, you will be more likely to remain mentally, emotionally, & spiritually healthy over the long haul.

The writer of Psalms says, "Those who know your name will trust in you, for you, Lord, have never forsaken those who seek you." (Psalm 9.10)

2. It has been said that the way to make God laugh is to tell him your plans. Why? God often changes them. He orchestrates & arranges what is best for you because he's aware of things you're not.

Remember what the Apostle Paul teaches us? "He knows us far better than we know ourselves... and keeps us present before God. That's why we can be so sure that every detail in our lives of love for God is worked into something good. God knew what he was doing from the very beginning. He decided from the outset to shape the lives of those who love him." (Romans 8.28-29)

Challenge: Think about a time when plans changed in your life – how did it result in something positive or beneficial?

Prayer: Lord, help me to trust you when plans change in my life so that I can adapt. Also, I ask you to help me see the benefits of my new direction. Amen.

Finding God in the Loss of Innocence
by April Carter

On January 28, 1999, doctors lay a tiny black haired, brown-eyed baby boy upon my chest. They kept referring to me as "mom," but at 17 years old I still needed my mom. For my mom it was the same hospital, same age, same situation, 17 years earlier. Most girls my age were getting ready for the winter dance, sports tryouts and class finals. I was getting ready to carry the weight of a choice I had made nine months earlier.

My whole world was shaken. I went from naïve teenager to responsible adult overnight. I had no idea how to raise a child. I was a child. I had plans to go to college on a softball scholarship and become a cop or a lawyer, not a teenage mother.

I knew God, well at least I thought I did. I went to church almost every Sunday my entire life. I sat through message after message, prayer after prayer. How was I so lost? How did I get here?

The Bible says in Matthew 18.12, "If a man has a hundred sheep and one of them wanders away, what will he do? Won't he leave the ninety-nine others on the hills and go out and search for the one that is lost?"

It doesn't take much for a sheep to wander away. Keep your head down long enough consumed by life's disappointments, distractions, and desires and you'll be lost too. I wandered far from God. I thought I was where

115

I was supposed to be all along, but my internal GPS must have been way off.

I was being led by pain, disappointment and various voids in my life. In the midst of my wandering, God pursued me and rescued me. When he found me, I wasn't the fluffiest and cuddliest of all sheep. I was dirty, humiliated, depressed and full of rage. He took the weight I had been carrying and put it upon his shoulders and brought me back to the place he longed for me to be.

Even in the darkest places of our lives, God is relentlessly pursuing us. He's not trying to hurt or punish us. He longs to bring us back into a right relationship with him.

Are there circumstances in your life that you have allowed to distract you from the goodness of God?

Question: Have you ever wandered from God and asked yourself, "How'd I get here?"

Prayer: Jesus, help me to keep my eyes on you and not wander from you even when painful situations and circumstances arise.

Finding God in the Bathroom
by Kristen Loehrmann

And the Holy Spirit helps us in our weakness... We don't know what to pray for. But the Holy Spirit prays for us with groanings that cannot be expressed in words. — Romans 8.26

We'd just arrived to explore Leavenworth when Eric started looking ill.

"I, uh..." he stammered and fished around in his pocket. After a mere six months of dating I could not have expected what he now held in his hand. "I wanted to wait until after dinner, but I can't. Will you marry me?"

Now it was my turn to look ill. Though it had been three years ago, I went through a painful separation, and the thought of marrying again terrified me. Especially since I wasn't certain where this boyfriend of mine stood on his beliefs. I knew he believed in God, "but so does Satan," my mother would say.

"It's lovely," I tried buying time. He looked so hopeful. I handed him back the ring, "But no..."

He stood. I stammered. He questioned. I reassured. He shut down. I reasoned. He suggested dinner. I suggested wine.

In the bathroom, freshening up, I looked into the mirror and saw a woman who looked like she'd been lost just long enough not to remember where the road was; like

117

someone who needed a Savior. "Lord," I prayed silently. "I have no idea what I'm doing. I need you to help me…" I had no other words.

After swallowing a strained dinner and the knowledge that we were to share a room – and a bed – for the next two days, we decided to make the best of it with an expensive bottle of cabernet. And when that was gone, the Jacuzzi looked like a good idea. I owed it to him, didn't I?

Except suddenly it seemed like a very bad idea.

Looking back, I can still picture the room, the bathroom where I prayed, the tub with a mound of bubbles, the down comforter. And I can still hear His voice: "You need to get a few things straight, child. Then we'll talk."

"Then we'll talk?" I shooed the voice away as if it was a fruit fly. "Get some things straight." Whatever that meant.

Then, more insistently: "If you cannot even submit to Me, how will you ever submit in marriage?"

"I'll be right back," I said.

Nowhere in my vocabulary was the word "submit." Nowhere had I heard this voice before. I couldn't blame the wine. I had prayed for help, and my answer came at what seemed like the very worst time…

Today we still laugh about the weekend that changed us both. After several months apart, when Eric told me he wanted to meet this God of mine "who talks to people in the bathroom" we started praying together. Sometimes we still don't even have the words to pray. But twelve years of marriage later, I know I will trust Him when he speaks.

Question: When has God been present to you in a moment of your life that would seem least likely for him to show up?

Prayer: Lord, help me to hear and obey the voice of your Spirit – even when I don't feel like it.

FINDING GOD

ABOUT THE AUTHOR/EDITOR

Brian Dolleman and his wife Shari have been the Lead Pastors of NWLife Church in Renton, WA since 2007. They both grew up in the Seattle area and love the Northwest. They've been married for 20 years, have been in ministry together for 20 years, and have a 13 year old daughter, Ashah. Brian is committed to building a church for the prodigals—a safe place, with a grace-filled "welcome home" message. Brian has been so personally touched by the incredible grace of our loving God, he had "Changed by Grace" tattooed on his arm. Brian Dolleman blogs & podcasts regularly on his website: www.northwestleader.com